Printed in Great Britain
by Amazon

32825205R00059